How to Succeed in the Vocation of Marriage

in

THIS CHAOTIC WORLD

Driving Your Purpose While Sailing Away from Adversity

HEIDI ARNONE, MS

*A book about finding joy and patience
in marriage and parenting while
navigating this chaotic world!*

DKL FOREVER
Clyde, Michigan

Graphic design and book packaging services provided by FastEditing LLC, Jeanette Fast Redmond, Owner, www.fastediting.biz.

ISBN-13 (print): 979-8-89496-240-5
ISBN-13 (ebook): 979-8-89496-249-8

First printing, July 2024

This book is lovingly dedicated to all in the marriage vocation and with the honor of parenting. It is to be passed on to the unborn of generations yet to come. May you forgive your past mistakes and become relentless in your driven purpose! The most gratitude is given to God the Father, the Son, and the Holy Spirit along with the Church. I give credit to my spouse, children, parents, and in-laws for passing on the faith, and to my family, friends, and local community for your continuous encouragement driving me forward to sail away from adversity!

When the parents had gone out and shut the door of the room, Tobias got out of bed and said to Sarah, "Sister, get up, and let us pray and implore our Lord that he grant us mercy and safety." So she got up, and they began to pray and implore that they might be kept safe. Tobias began by saying,

"Blessed are you, O God of our ancestors,
     and blessed is your name in all
          generations forever.
Let the heavens and the whole
     creation bless you forever.
You made Adam, and for him you
     made his wife Eve
     as a helper and support.
     From the two of them the human
          race has sprung.
You said, 'It is not good that the
     man should be alone;
     let us make a helper for him like himself.'
I now am taking this kinswoman of mine,
     not because of lust,
     but with sincerity.
Grant that she and I may find mercy
     and that we may grow old together."

And they both said, "Amen, Amen."

—TOBIT 8:4-8 (NRSVCE)

Contents

Stay in Good Air and Go the Distance

Have You Ever Wondered
How to Sail into Your Dreams?

Have you found yourself in search of who you are? Do you wear many hats? Do you wonder what direction to take?

If so, you're not alone. Staying focused on past moments can keep your mind captive, unable to engage with the present moment, and can prevent you from moving forward. We all have different distractions fighting for our attention constantly. What's important is that you follow your internal compass to lead you in the direction God is calling you to go.

Scientists have determined that our heart valves are one of the last organs to go upon our death. Be humble of heart, rather than just doing what others request of you. Indeed, you are better served by following your gut, as it makes all the difference in attitude. Although it is certainly good to serve your neighbor when you are able, as individuals we are walking a path of finding belonging and significance. As the Old Testament book of Ecclesiastes reminds us, there is a time for all things through our seasons of existence. Below, and throughout this book, you will find scriptural verses to support the timeless story of man and woman's journey together since the very beginning of human creation.

For everything there is a season, and a time
       for every matter under heaven:
a time to be born, and a time to die;
a time to plant, and a time to pluck
       up what is planted;
a time to kill, and a time to heal;
a time to break down, and a time to build up;
a time to weep, and a time to laugh;
a time to mourn, and a time to dance;
a time to throw away stones, and a time
       to gather stones together;
a time to embrace, and a time to
       refrain from embracing;
a time to seek, and a time to lose;
a time to keep, and a time to throw away;
a time to tear, and a time to sew;
a time to keep silence, and a time to speak;
a time to love, and a time to hate;
a time for war, and a time for peace.

—ECCLESIASTES 3:1-8

Be vigilant about judging a book by its cover. We never know what another individual might be facing, or we could be hit with hardship ourselves.

Have you ever heard yourself saying "I'm too old" or "I can't do this"? Maybe you have even heard someone close to you say such things—such as your spouse, kids, parents, grandchildren, co-workers, administrators, friends, or acquaintances. These self-limiting beliefs only hold you back from becoming the "you" that you want to be.

As humans, we can become what we think through the words we speak over ourselves. You can look yourself by narrowing credible internet searches for people who have experienced great success doing things into old age. Some examples you could search for include longest marriage, oldest college graduate, starting a business in later years, or writing a book.

When creating the best version of yourself, you can be different from the norm. It's okay. If you fall, get back up and try again. Through failure we gain experience to perfect our efforts in the future.

> The Lord is gracious and merciful,
>   slow to anger and abounding
>   in steadfast love.
> The Lord is good to all,
> and his compassion is over all
>   that he has made.
> All your works shall give thanks
>   to you, O Lord,

and all your faithful shall bless you. . . .
The eyes of all look to you,
and you give them their food
in due season. . . .
The Lord is just in all his ways,
and kind in all his doings.
The Lord is near to all who call on him,
to all who call on him in truth.

—PSALM 145:8-10, 15, 17-18 (NRSVCE)

Leave the Dock, Raise Your Sails, and Move Faster Than the Storm

CHAPTER 1

Forming Alliance in Your Marriage

Have you ever felt like you're being pulled every which way by people inside and outside your household? How about feeling distracted from your intentions for the day?

You're definitely not alone with these thoughts. But it's time you start driving your purpose so you can sail away from past wounds. At times you may feel like no matter how much you do or take on, it's never enough. The people you surround yourself with are never pleased. These thoughts can lead you to call on the Lord. Remember: You are not walking this journey alone, and you're enough just the way you are! Jesus died on the Cross to forgive our sins. You have done nothing that can't be healed through our relationship with him.

> I will instruct you and teach you
> the way you should go;
> I will counsel you with my eye upon you.
>
> —PSALM 32:8 (NRSVCE)

Trust in the Lord with all your heart,
and do not rely on your own insight.
In all your ways acknowledge him,
and he will make straight your paths.

—PROVERBS 3:5-6 (NRSVCE)

Wanting to help others is a great reason to find your calling. Whenever we call on our Creator, the Lord, he guides us in better ways than we can follow ourselves. So when you follow his paths, he will help you lose deadly tribulations such as anger, depression, ego, envy, fear, gluttony, greed, jealousy, laziness, lies, lust, and poverty. And becoming free of these temptations will lead you to your determined purpose.

For example, your dream might be to lose weight—but dig deeper. Why do you want to lose weight? Is it because you want to break bondage to food and live a long life? Or maybe you don't want to count on others as you age. Maybe you have never felt confident getting up and speaking in front of a crowd, but you could aspire to do that now, or any other goal that is prompting you to lose weight. Try to understand where your desire comes from, and then surrender yourself to the Lord. He will shine a light to lead you out of the darkness.

> There are six things that the Lord hates,
>   seven that are an abomination to him:
> haughty eyes, a lying tongue,
>   and hands that shed innocent blood,
> a heart that devises wicked plans,
>   feet that hurry to run to evil,
> a lying witness who testifies falsely,
>   and one who sows discord in a family.
>
> —PROVERBS 6:16-19 (NRSVCE)

Families who pray and play together are more likely to stay together. Husbands and wives can model this understanding with their children by taking part in activities together. You and your spouse can build your faith together and create unity in your marriage vocation through a multitude of ways. Most importantly, you can give back to your community by volunteering, especially through your church; if you are Catholic, you can attend Eucharistic Adoration, the Sacrament of Reconciliation, and daily Mass together.

If you don't yet have a relationship with God yet, or it's just forming, start small. If you're unable to get your spouse on board, you can add and build upon your daily habits. Modeling them will offer encouragement to those around you.

Consider this list of suggestions to unify your marriage and build more connection:

1. Go to church together. Start small by going to Sunday Mass (even if it's Saturday night), and then add daily Mass when time allows.

2. Learn a new hobby or skill together. Time apart is great as well, but when you come together with your spouse, you create more unity through the five senses: sight, hearing, touch, taste, smell, and feel.

3. Travel and explore a new place together. Try new restaurants or vacations. Break old traditions and be open to change. It certainly can be comforting to keep things the same, but this sameness limits your ability to grow. Be open to learning something new.

4. Dance together, even in your own home with nobody else watching.

5. Exercise with each other. You can motivate each other by suggesting a walk, or maybe just doing yard work together. Threats or force are never encouraging. If your partner has limited time, just start small by sharing how you like to spend quality time together.

6. Read a book together, preferably something to strengthen marriage and the family. Again, if your spouse has limited time, you can model

this idea by being in their presence and reading a book yourself. If your spouse prefers to watch TV at the end of the day to unwind, sit near them while you read your book and they watch TV.

7. Cook a new recipe together, perhaps with your own twist.

8. Serve others together. Volunteer with your spouse, and perhaps include your children. Volunteering through your church is a great way to do this, or look for local community events as well.

9. Have open and sincere discussions with each other, even if it hurts to hear the truth. Try to take honesty as constructive criticism and work on your faults. If you're not ready to hear what your spouse has to say, you can set boundaries, but be sure to do so with a calm voice. This will invite God into your marriage.

Healthy competition in a marriage can encourage each of you to do what is right. Be sure to focus on the positive things your spouse is doing for you, and give praise if you want to see more of these in your life. Avoid your spouse's negative comments to reduce hearing criticism. Recognizing the little things goes a long way. Be sure to say thank you when your spouse does a task that you usually do yourself, and let them know how helpful they were. Always give credit where it is due.

Therefore encourage one another and build
up each other, as indeed you are doing.

—1 THESSALONIANS 5:11 (NRSVCE)

If you are seeking help with your marriage, talk about it with those with marriage "skills": others who have joy and marital bliss in their own lives. They will display the fruits of the Holy Spirit.

By contrast, the fruit of the Spirit is love,
joy, peace, patience, kindness, generosity,
faithfulness, gentleness, and self-control.
There is no law against such things.

—GALATIANS 5:22-23 (NRSVCE)

You don't have to walk alone. Before marriage, talk with your partner about ways you wish to form your union and unity. One idea is to list the things you hope to pass on to future generations together, or things each of you desires to do differently from what was passed on to you. These discussions can be challenging if you were brought up in different environments or faiths, but you will only benefit if you come to a meeting of the minds for your future desires. Remember, no matter how much you plan, your intentions won't always work out as you envision. But letting things happen more organically, versus always planning them in advance, can free you from stress and allow greater euphoria. It's okay to set boundaries in advance, if you can anticipate them; but certainly you will find it best to handle any situation head-on, as it is happening in the present.

Becoming one in marriage is essential for your continued growth. First you must learn each other's personalities to see how you can encourage and strengthen one another. Learning each other's tenderness of heart is extremely beneficial. You can build each other up through offering positive words, giving gifts, serving one another through acts of kindness, spending quality time together, or offering tangible touch such as hugs. Be sure to ask your partner what they most gravitate toward, rather than just assuming you know best.

> He answered, "Have you not read that the one who made them at the beginning 'made them male and female,' and said, 'For this reason a man shall leave his father and mother and be joined to his wife, and the two shall become one flesh'? So they are no longer two, but one flesh. Therefore what God has joined together, let no one separate."
>
> —MATTHEW 19:4-6 (NRSVCE)

When unifying your marriage, be open to learning new ways. This openness might require forgiving your past and truly submitting yourself to God. Submission means handing him your problem and asking him to fix it. To do this, you must relinquish comfort and power—otherwise known as control. Once you have surrendered yourself to God, remember there is no problem he cannot fix. Most importantly, avoid saying, "God can't fix this problem, so I take it back." Rather, close your eyes and put yourself in God's shoes by imagining yourself giving something to a close friend and then asking to have it back. Some things can be ingrained since childhood. It could be as simple as a household task such as folding the laundry, putting dishes in the washer, or celebrating holiday traditions. Doing something different might feel awkward at first, but it leads to growth in your marriage and helps you reprogram your self-limiting beliefs.

Forming unity through marriage can be an exciting time to grow, but it can also create melancholy thoughts from time to time. You can also find it challenging to face obstacles you have never endured. Maybe you even reflect on some things learned from your own parents or caregivers. For example, it's important for spouses to consider each other's differences. It's good to be open to learning new ways of trying something, even if they are different from what you have done in the past or were taught. Keeping peace in the family makes it crucial to meet in the middle, rather than just doing everything the way things were done in your past. Release some of your ego, and be open to change. A phrase you might find helpful is "Try a little something new." By doing so, you can expand your knowledge. You might find that there is more than one way to get similar results.

Jesus died on the Cross for our sins. No other person can be a god, but the purpose of your journey here is to be the best version of yourself. God had prophets and great followers, as he still does today, in this time. Worldly things and positions are always changing. That's why the rich are not always joyous. What matters is not the size of your house or number of children you have; rather, it is the love within your heart and your tenacious attitude, no matter what conditions you face. Through patience and understanding of this concept, your marriage will thrive. One thing is for certain: the love of our savior, Jesus Christ, who lives and reigns within each one of us.

Whenever you feel uncomfortable trying something for the first time, you can take it as a sure sign that you're growing in strength and out of weakness. Just think of a toddler facing lots of new milestones—take potty training, for example, and that fear of sitting on the potty for the first time and having multiple accidents. That toddler feels uncomfortable, but they face new challenges by continuing to try until they have success by going on the potty. They may even feel ashamed and weary—but they don't give up until they have flourished.

When you first set about forming unity in your marriage, embrace the now rather than holding on to traditions of the past.

Our pasts as human persons are certainly of value, as they hold great history and provide us with our sense of belonging in this earthly world, which leads to our identity or our call to the vocation of who we ultimately become. Remember the Church was founded on Peter the Apostle. That's why the priestly vocation in the Catholic faith is so needed—without priests we have no Church to pass on to future generations. (If you are blessed with a son, consider advocating for the vocation of priesthood. For more on this, you can contact a vocations director at your local Catholic parish or diocese to help with discernment.)

It is okay to remember the past. It is part of who you are today and part of who you have yet become. At the same time, the past can be challenging when you first come together as husband and wife and form unity. You might come from different or similar backgrounds. Regardless, remember that we all are more alike than we are different.

Take household chores like folding a towel. A towel can be folded in a multitude of ways. Sometimes breaking old habits or customs that have been passed on from previous generations can prevent you from struggling with your family now. Accept that there are different ways to complete tasks. Whatever works best for your situation might be opposite to how it was done in previous generations. The more you accept something the way it is, the more at peace you will be.

This suggestion also leads to the Golden Rule: treating others the way we want to be treated. This acceptance comes off as an act of kindness, rather than just "do it my way." Besides, who are we to judge? There is only one Creator. It is certainly okay to stand up for your beliefs and values, within reason, kindness to others is preferable versus displaying any form of anger or judgment.

> Put away from you all bitterness and wrath and anger and wrangling and slander, together with all malice, and be kind to one another, tenderhearted, forgiving one another, as God in Christ has forgiven you.
>
> —EPHESIANS 4:31-32 (NRSVCE)

> For if you forgive others their trespasses, your heavenly Father will also forgive you; but if you do not forgive others, neither will your Father forgive your trespasses.
>
> —MATTHEW 6:14-15 (NRSVCE)

> Love is patient; love is kind; love is not envious or boastful or arrogant or rude. It does not insist on its own way; it is not irritable or resentful; it does not rejoice in wrongdoing, but rejoices in the truth. It bears all things, believes all things, hopes all things, endures all things.
>
> —1 CORINTHIANS 13:4-7 (NRSVCE)

Most of all, when settling into your parent role, be sure to become the person God created you to be. It's okay if you've listened to your parents, teachers, and coaches who guided you along the way, as long as you become the person you're destined to be, as opposed to someone others told you to become.

Building a solid support system is essential. Support systems are important for both emotional and physical wellbeing, including emergency household repairs, babysitting, and advice as needed. Turning toward extended family members, friends, neighbors, teachers, mentors, and other parents—including your own—can be immensely helpful. As an African proverb says, "It takes a village to raise a child."

Two are better than one, because they have a good reward for their toil. For if they fall, one will lift up the other; but woe to one who is alone and falls and does not have another to help. Again, if two lie together, they keep warm; but how can one keep warm alone? And though one might prevail against another, two will withstand one. A threefold cord is not quickly broken.

—ECCLESIASTES 4:9-12 (NRSVCE)

CHAPTER 2

Creating Family Unity Between Husband and Wife

When establishing family unity, compromise as often as you can. Coming to terms most of the time helps others listen more when you truly do need to take a stand. This skill will help tremendously to grow your relationships in your home. Be sure to remember that it's okay to set boundaries to reach set goals and time frame targets. But by practicing what you preach, you model expected behaviors you wish to see in your family in the future.

Occasional differences are okay. These disputes are growing pains. It is good for children to witness how your marriage comes to a meeting of the minds, even when you disagree, as long as you do so peacefully. You are your child's number-one teacher, and it is good for them to see ways to give and take. When you strive for compromise, you're modeling how to be humble. It's okay to not always be right. Finding ways to come together promotes growth, and it can certainly be done while having fun.

> How very good and pleasant it is
> when kindred live together in unity!
>
> —PSALM 133:1 (NRSVCE)

Some suggestions for strengthening family unity include these points:

1. Schedule individual time with each family member, as we are all different. Even for big families, start with small windows of time frames, or get creative by pairing up other family members while you spend individual time with each child and your partner. Bedtime routines can be a great way to start this routine. Remember to start small and build on this as time goes on.

2. Share meals together, and be open to trying new things outside your comfort zone.

3. Do routine tasks like chores together. Avoid "my way" syndrome and be open to alternative ways to get similar results.

4. Create a family mission statement about things each family member feels passionate about, and be understanding of one another's values. Establish family traditions and work toward goals together.

5. Have weekly family meetings that you do not cancel. Meetings will help build communication

skills among your family as you listen to what family members say.

6. Encourage and support one another through inspirations that point to what each person does well.

7. Be sure to schedule downtime and show gratitude for your blessings.

8. Volunteer together as a group, or with individual family members. With children, split your time equally to avoid any sibling rivalry.

9. Keep a master calendar of daily and weekly family activities so you don't create schedule conflicts and can work out transportation.

10. As a caregiver or parent, stay consistent with daily habits, and be sure to use patience.

Everyday, mundane tasks probably pull your attention constantly. To maintain unity within the family home, check in daily:

- Check in with each other both at morning and at night.

- Be sure to say goodbye through some form of physical touch, such as a hug, before parting for the day, as well as hugging to say hello when reuniting.

- Follow up throughout the day through quick texts or voice notes to let your family members know you're thinking of them. You can mention things that made you think of them, such as "I saw [something] and it reminded me of you."

- Greet each other when you reunite later in the day, and spend a few minutes recapping each other's days.

- Be sure to show up for each other, physically and emotionally.

- Limit distractions by blocking out technology or other interruptions. During device-free time, offer undivided attention. You can pray together, cook, eat meals together, read together, or engage in other activities together.

As a parent you must model within yourself the behaviors you wish to see in your family. Remember that it's okay to make mistakes and not be perfect. Just have understanding when others do the same. Have you ever heard of the saying "Practice what you preach"? How can you expect your children to do something that you're not willing to do yourself? Oftentimes parents forget that children make mistakes and that it's important to be accepting of their faults. Your job as a parent is to guide them and lead them to the truth. Encourage them by showing them how to get back up when they fall—and yes, they will fall. Remember that accidents happen and that's okay, as long as the mistake isn't repeated going forward.

When teaching your children, foster independence if a task is something they can do for themselves. For example, if your child has already mastered a task and tries to get you to do it for them, stay consistent in having them continue their independence for growth. Otherwise you will find them regressing to previous stages, out of which you have already trained them, and will essentially cost more of your time. Sometimes as the parent, you may find it easier to just do a task for them and save time. But in the long term, this solution doesn't teach them how to do it for themselves or to become independent from you. After all, your job is to train them in the way they should go. Time flies faster than you think, so enjoy every moment; you have only a limited number of chances to spend time with your children. This holds true even if you are a stay-at-home parent, as you complete other tasks to keep up your home.

Parenting while maintaining family unity is extremely important to keep the family together. Being great parents doesn't always mean being in the spotlight or getting recognized. It means coming together as one, even for things that don't go the way you would like. You must be open to new ideas and be willing to take constructive criticism.

The thing about parenting is we have lots of ways to respond to situations. Most important is that you are forging a connection between you and your child to love unconditionally. You have lots of different options to lead a child in the direction they should go. You can model your values through the words you speak, your attitude, and the actions you take. Being consistent, being disciplined, and establishing boundaries are good rules to live by and will help you connect with your family. Focusing on a child's positive actions is a good way to encourage them to repeat those behaviors in the future. Stepping back and letting natural consequences play out also fosters responsibility in the long term. Seeing your child fail can be difficult; but failure ultimately leads to future victory, and it is a good prevention to ward against future entitlement or privilege. Failure also builds great character and strength. One of the purposes of parenting is to lead your child to become productive in their adult years and draw closer to Jesus. Live a fruitful life that is passed onto future generations.

> Now, discipline always seems painful rather than pleasant at the time, but later it yields the peaceful fruit of righteousness to those who have been trained by it.
>
> —HEBREWS 12:11 (NRSVCE)

CHAPTER 3

Caring for Children and Passing on the Faith

As a caregiver, you must be there when your child needs you. Especially if there are safety concerns, one way to create a safe environment with a child is to develop a daily routine. Even if you don't do things at the same time each day, pick tasks and routines that are unchangeable or nonadjustable, such as bedtime during the school week, healthy diet choices or food combinations, and safety concerns. Although it is normal to slip from these disciplines, just remember consistency is usually best. Both children and adults feel safe when they have structure and know what is expected of them.

Avoid giving too many consequences or ultimatums to avoid hearing rude remarks, also known as backtalk. Children need to feel your presence to build their personal relationship and trust with you. Be sure to avoid terrorizing and yelling, which always leads to anger, fear, and self-doubt. Such reactions will also teach your kids to react similarly to situations.

Acting the same way over time plays a valuable role in raising children. Especially when fighting sleep battles, technology wars, and homework struggles, creating and setting contracts and shared understandings can be helpful. Keeping up with your children's interests will help you stay relevant to what is current. Be sure to stick to any rules you set, and avoid caving in. Kids do remember and will test you the next time, if you don't stay firm. It's easy to give in temporarily, as it provides relief. But longer-term, giving in has more effects producing the behaviors you wish not to see. When you invest the time up front, you help your child come to terms with what you expect of them going onward.

When working on connections with your children, be fully present by turning off or tuning out any distractions. Doing so promotes what you want them to mirror back: undivided attention. This approach creates a strong bond through listening to what is being said. Make this part of your everyday routine. This time should also not be shared. If you're the only adult in the home during this one-on-one time, then set up your other children with another activity until you can spend time with them next. Be sure not to skip out on this strategy, or negative behaviors could occur, because negative attention is better than no attention at all. A good starting point might be spending 5 to 10 minutes with each child, depending on how many you have and what your time allows.

If you are getting ready for company, or you have an important task for work, spend this time with your children before taking care of your other obligation, as a way to encourage more patience on the child's part. When spending individual time with a child, be sure not to lecture or teach during this time. Try to get on their level so they look at you more as a peer than authority figure. This approach will help build your connection with them.

When they are in a dangerous situation, they will be more likely to take any parental criticism as Gospel. When a child's feelings are hurt, they are likely to respond in the most negative ways. So spending that individual time can really increase their positive behaviors.

If a child is giving you a lot of impertinence, their feelings more than likely feel threatened. The best thing you can do in this situation is avoid any form of punishment, which just comes across as hostile and provokes cynical conduct. Any consequence like this will just get the child to shut down and feel hopeless. For example, consider a child who lacks growth in education or has poor confidence in any hobby, whether sports or other extracurricular activities. A quick way to build confidence is to spend individual time and offer more choice. This allows the child to feel more unconditional love through reconnecting with you and allows forgiveness of any past wrongdoings.

As a parent you want to promote your children's independence. Your main purposes as a parent are to guide your child, protect them from harm, and support them by providing food, shelter, and clothing. Encourage your children to move forward in development and growth. Motivate them to become self-doers who can care for their own needs, versus having to count on others. Inspire them to fully read or listen to directions or instructions before asking questions. This lesson fosters single-mindedness and keeps them steadfast. Most of the time, when we are patient as opposed to being anxious, our question will be answered in due time.

If your child is demonstrating a sense of entitlement, it might be time to shift their mindset. Children are often learning things for the first time or from a new perspective. So go easy on them and avoid lecturing. A key phrase is "Now you know for next time." By reflecting kindness you will be more likely to receive it back. Remember that what goes around comes around!

Caring for both children and aging parents at the same time means taking even greater leadership and stepping in at the most inconvenient times. It might mean losing sleep or committing to tasks you didn't plan for. It means experiencing massive pressures if you aren't careful with setting boundaries. When something goes wrong, you must hold back from yelling or screaming, even though this is very tempting, and instead encourage them to try again.

A soft answer turns away wrath,
>   but a harsh word stirs up anger.

—PROVERBS 15:1 (NRSVCE)

For all must carry their own loads.

—GALATIANS 6:5 (NRSVCE)

When helping your family, you might find it difficult to endure at times. You might feel like you are doing more for them than caring for your own needs. In such times it is okay to evaluate the situation and slow yourself down. Doing so does not mean that you won't help or be available to your loved ones. Rather, setting limits just means you're not available in the current moment but will become available after you have cared for your own needs. Let your family know that you really want to listen or help when you are done with your current mission. Let them know you have to complete another task but will follow up after. Then be certain to follow up as you said you would. This follow-through helps build trust, furthering your relationship by being accountable.

Let me briefly share a small part of my personal testimony about furthering your relationship through personal accountability. Obstacles began in my own marriage shortly after we said our "I do's." We conceived our first child four months into our marriage—only to find out halfway through the pregnancy, during the anatomy scan, that our precious daughter's body wasn't developing correctly. Some of the organs, including her heart, appeared to be located outside her body. At the time the hospital told us that she was "incompatible with life" and advised us to have her terminated to reduce future risks with other potential pregnancies—as if the diagnosis weren't enough already. This hospital considered itself religion-based.

This diagnosis left us in the angst of where to turn and who to confide in. Our research revealed that a couple similar cases reportedly survived, but survival was extremely rare and included a risk of severe physical handicaps. But the anatomy report from the hospital could not say for certain that the baby would die or had a 0% chance of survival. The words the report used to describe the anomalies were "appears" or "looks like." Without any certainty, how could I end her life? After all I did not form this child in my womb—so who was I to make this call?

> Before I formed you in the womb I knew you,
> and before you were born I consecrated you;
> I appointed you a prophet to the nations.
>
> —JEREMIAH 1:5 (NRSVCE)

My husband is a "cradle Catholic," and I came to Catholicism as a teenager—and neither of us had the slightest idea of what to do next. Having a social work background myself, I knew the best thing was to take some time before making any rash decisions, as I'd have to live with my final choice for the rest of my life. Through prayer and lots of discernment, we came to the decision to put in God's hands whatever was meant to be. I knew that if I terminated the baby myself, I would always carry thoughts of "what if": what if a miracle might have happened, and I ended our baby's life too soon? With utmost shattering we found out a few weeks later that our precious baby's heartbeat was lost in the womb. I no longer felt the pressure to make a decision to terminate the pregnancy, as our precious little girl's life had naturally ended.

It's not that God doesn't forgive us for our sins through his grace and mercy. He sent Jesus to die on the Cross at Calvary for our sins. We have a choice to call on him or to turn away from him through our own free will. During and after that pregnancy, I questioned God's love in my life. I turned away from the Church, thinking, "How could he do this to me?" Anger and darkness filled my heart. I blamed God for what happened and took it out on my surroundings for a number of years.

But as more time has passed, I have realized God's mercy in my life. Through the gift of reconciliation, he has blessed my marriage with three beautiful children after our loss. We can't be prouder of and grateful for our children. My desire is to pass on the faith: to them, and to the generations yet to come.

My healing journey started when I turned back to my faith and had sincere repentance. Personally I came to the conclusion that it's not just "my body, my choice"—it's the baby's life as well. The Right For Life and Heartbeat International stand for a human's right to live without another entity making decisions. Some studies have found that abortion can play a pivotal role on a woman's mental health, psychological well being, and have possible risk for fertility issues with future pregnancies. If you find yourself in a similar situation, you might take comfort in the Sacrament of Reconciliation, as many have reported experiencing such comfort during great trials in their lives. There are of course ongoing opposing stances involving this claim of "my body, my choice."

The *Catechism of the Catholic Church*, paragraph 2271, teaches us:

> Since the first century the Church has affirmed the moral evil of every procured abortion. This teaching has not changed and remains unchangeable. Direct abortion, that is to say, abortion willed either as an end or a means, is gravely contrary to the moral law: "You shall not kill the embryo by abortion and shall not cause the newborn to perish." "God, the Lord of life, has entrusted to men the noble mission of safeguarding life, and men must carry it out in a manner worthy

of themselves. Life must be protected with the utmost care from the moment of conception: abortion and infanticide are abominable crimes."[*]

Our experience taught me how to rely more on my faith than my own understanding. As human beings, we aren't always right; we make errors. When we call on Jesus through prayer, we are counting on him for our salvation. Throughout the Bible, we are told not to be afraid or anxious about anything. This reminder certainly doesn't mean you can pray once to God and have him take away your worries. Rather, developing a relationship through daily supplication and gratitude will change your heart. Another great option is to join Bible studies to further your knowledge.

As indicated by the story I shared, you must remember to use your faith and morals as a guiding light. In situations related to your spouse and raising children, there is no set way to place boundaries— so do what works best for your family. You might explain decisions that apply just for that moment in time, to avoid disagreements down the road. It's also okay to remind your spouse and kids that what worked in the past may no longer be relevant. Staying present is a good way to determine what's expected and avoid major accidents.

---

[*] *Catechism of the Catholic Church*, 2nd ed. (Washington, DC: United States Conference of Catholic Bishops, 2001), no. 2271, quoting *Didache* 2, 2: SCh 248, 148; cf. Ep. Barnabae 19, 5: PG 2, 777; *Ad Diognetum* 5, 6: PG 2, 1173; Tertullian, Apol. 9: PL 1, 319-320; and also quoting Second Vatican Council, *Gaudium et Spes*, no. 51.3.

Take time to train your children. Especially in today's world, when it comes to technology, be sure to instruct your children in appropriate uses. This instruction helps ensure the safety of your children. You can also discuss things with your children such as screen time limits and how they have a positive or negative impact on them. For instance, if your child has been waking you up in the middle of the night, it might be time to reduce screen usage in general and evaluate what specifically they are watching. Reviewing search histories and setting parental controls can be helpful ways to set age-appropriate boundaries. You can avoid future struggles through creating agreements that both parties approve for going forward. These will be important to review as situations change.

It's best to start training your children from early on, but don't beat yourself up if you have ignored it in the past. What matters is that you start setting boundaries now for the safety of your child. As children age, they are more likely to turn to peers for advice, so who they associate with can have an impact on their behaviors. You are certainly encouraged to teach your children to be accepting of all people, but it's okay to call out when someone is doing something you believe to be wrong. By teaching children these skills from a young age, you help them gain courage to stand up for themselves when something doesn't feel right. This courage will help them avoid long-term suffering.

CHAPTER 4

Giving Back to Your Community and Staying Present in Your Child's Educational Growth

Community events are one of the best opportunities to make new friends or build existing connections and relationships. You and your family can give back in a number of ways, such as volunteering time or offering funds through donations and even online giving. Not only does volunteering help others, but it can also help relieve your own stress. Volunteering has been known to reduce thoughts or symptoms of depression. Whether you give time, money, or talent, give only what you feel called to give. Don't worry about what others ask for—do what you personally value and believe in. You will feel calm, instead of feeling stressed by being pushed into something you aren't passionate about.

> Each of you must give as you have made
> up your mind, not reluctantly or under
> compulsion, for God loves a cheerful giver.
>
> —2 CORINTHIANS 9:7 (NRSVCE)

Manage your time wisely, as we are given just a short window on this earth. Delegating tasks through your support system can help you become more productive by freeing up more time. Remember that it's okay to say no rather than flood your schedule so that you barely have a chance to breathe throughout your day. Shut off or limit distractions so you can keep focused on the task at hand. Although multitasking can seem like you're getting more done at once, staying focused on one task is better. Grouping similar activities can lead to daily wins, which in turn can help you gain momentum toward your desired outcomes. Such clustering also keeps your brain focused on similar topics, to prevent it from jumping around to things that aren't relevant to the present moment.

Have you ever felt like others constantly ask for your help? You're not alone in having these thoughts. Be cautious with overthinking, which can be a mind trap for attracting negative emotions or thoughts. Rather, remind yourself that you can't control what others think about you—but you can control how you respond to situations, by letting others know what you're able to do. It's okay to say, "I'm not able to take that on at the moment, but I am able to [insert here what you can do]," "Please reach out again in the future," or "I'm not able to at this time, but I will let you know if something changes."

When you work with others in your community, avoid assuming what needs to be done. When making a commitment to help others, do things the way you are asked to do them, if you want to be treated with the same respect. If uncertain, ask rather than assume or guess. This strategy helps to leash your thoughts and avoid the imprisonment of negative thoughts. If you make a mistake, remember it's okay; consider it a growing pain. Take it as a valuable lesson and move forward.

In your community, get to know and be a part of ecumenical teams. These groups of people represent various churches that work together in unity for the greater good of everyone in the community.

Another form of giving back in your community is to serve other families or people in your neighborhood. Inviting them over is a great way to form closer relationships. You are able to come together in unity, and you might discover ways to benefit one another, such as carpooling to get kids to and from activities, picking up groceries, helping the elderly with yard work, or exchanging things like outgrown clothes, toys, babysitting services, house sitting help, or pet care.

> In all this I have given you an example that by such work we must support the weak, remembering the words of the Lord Jesus, for he himself said, "It is more blessed to give than to receive."
>
> —ACTS 20:35 (NRSVCE)

Be sure to stay involved in your child's education, whether you do so in person or from home. Your involvement helps them thrive in growth. Today a lot of teachers are communicating through technology. Teachers stay connected via apps, mobile texts, videos, and emailed summaries and other alerts. This outreach is helpful to help parents stay updated on what is happening throughout your child's day and about their behavioral progress. Be sure to follow up with your child to build more connections and show you take an interest in their day when you are apart. These new communication technologies are giving parents a profound look into their children's performance and experience in the classroom, while forging tighter relationships between educators and families. These apps have been great for keeping current with urgent replies for things such as snow days or other emergency situations.

*Correct Course by
Paying Attention to
Your Surroundings*

CHAPTER 5

Finding Health Through Meditation

Bringing awareness to the present moment can help you eliminate anxiety and stress. Looking at your calendar of planned events certainly can be overwhelming. But focusing on one thing at a time allows you to live in the here and now. For example, notice what is happening currently, not distractions from the past or future. Practicing being in the present helps with focus and the completion of desired tasks. Time goes fast, especially when caught up in the daily grind.

The words we speak in our lives make an impact on our thoughts. The power of our words can either build us up or weigh us down. So a good daily habit is to speak positivity in your life. Even if you don't currently feel positive, trying to focus on speaking positivity can play into your mood. Daily positive statements and affirmations can have a more profound impact on your day.

Speak positive statements out loud, not silently to yourself. This practice can be as simple as looking in a mirror first thing in the morning and saying them aloud. Another way is to write them in a notepad and read it aloud daily (or multiple times throughout your day), or record yourself and review the audio. These principles can help you increase confidence in yourself and build courage to be open to change.

> It is not what goes into the mouth that defiles a person, but it is what comes out of the mouth that defiles.
>
> —MATTHEW 15:11 (NRSVCE)

> Let no evil talk come out of your mouths, but only what is useful for building up, as there is need, so that your words may give grace to those who hear.
>
> —EPHESIANS 4:29 (NRSVCE)

> Pleasant words are like a honeycomb,
> sweetness to the soul and
> health to the body.
>
> —PROVERBS 16:24 (NRSVCE)

Some other suggestions for building wellness through meditation and prayer are the following:

- Bring awareness to the present by surrendering yourself to Jesus. Ask him to show you things from your past that need healing.

- Develop and strengthen your creativity and imagination. Be optimistic by trying new things to grow. Be open to hearing the Word of God by attracting positivity in your surroundings.

- Reduce your negative emotions and thoughts by repeating positive words to yourself and loved ones. You can do this through daily consistent prayer types: petition, intercession, praise, thanksgiving, and blessing.

- Develop alternative ways to respond to challenges and reduce your stress levels. It's okay to say no or limit your availability by working on yourself. When you slow things down, you draw closer to God.

- Another great method is fasting—which doesn't necessarily mean fasting from food. Think of things in your life that you need to limit so you can better hear God's Word.

- Meditate and dream upon the future you wish to see in your life. Print pictures or put positive quotes around your environment as daily reminders of your wishes and desires. This strategy will help change your attitude and draw your relationships closer.

- Attend weekly or even daily Mass for more healing, and confess your sins regularly in the Sacrament of Reconciliation. The more you do this, the closer you will draw to Jesus.

- Forgive your past by envisioning Jesus as coming to you personally and saying, "I love you." Remember that those who can forgive their neighbor will be forgiven themselves.

> For if you forgive others their trespasses, your heavenly Father will also forgive you.
>
> —MATTHEW 6:14 (NRSVCE)

Scriptures to Meditate On

You can use any of the Scripture passages in this book to prompt your own contemplation and meditation. Here are some additional passages about wisdom, knowledge, perseverance, and patience.

> Happy are those who find wisdom, and those who get understanding.
>
> —PROVERBS 3:13 (NRSVCE)

For "no human being will be justified in his sight" by deeds prescribed by the law, for through the law comes the knowledge of sin.

But now, apart from law, the righteousness of God has been disclosed, and is attested by the law and the prophets, the righteousness of God through faith in Jesus Christ for all who believe. For there is no distinction, since all have sinned and fall short of the glory of God; they are now justified by his grace as a gift, through the redemption that is in Christ Jesus.

—ROMANS 3:20-24 (NRSVCE)

Rejoice in hope, be patient in suffering, persevere in prayer.

—ROMANS 12:12 (NRSVCE)

Let this be recorded for a generation to come, so that a people yet unborn may praise the LORD.

—PSALM 102:18 (NRSVCE)

CHAPTER 6

Reading the Word of God Leads to Positive Growth

A daily reading habit offers many benefits. If you're not an avid reader of daily Scripture, then find another topic that interests you as a way to build skill. The Holy Bible is one of the most widely read books. This passage from Revelation refers specifically to that book but can be understood as referring to the entire Word of God.

> I warn everyone who hears the words of the prophecy of this book: if anyone adds to them, God will add to that person the plagues described in this book; if anyone takes away from the words of the book of this prophecy, God will take away that person's share in the tree of life and in the holy city, which are described in this book.
>
> —REVELATION 22:18-19 (NRSVCE)

You don't always have to learn from your own mistakes. You can also learn from reading about the mistakes of others, described in fiction and nonfiction alike. Reading strengthens a lot of skills, such as your vocabulary, and connects you to others. Ultimately reading leads to worthwhile relationships.

Reading is a good way to expand your knowledge. Reading frequently can also help increase your vocabulary by exposing you to more words. Being well spoken can build self-esteem and confidence toward the work you do. Some researchers believe that reading even helps you live longer. Reading certainly improves critical thinking and focus. It improves communication skills among people and is believed to reduce stress by strengthening the memory.

Pinpoint where you want to see growth in your life. Researching the topic and reading books on that subject will strengthen your knowledge and educate you on ways to become a lifelong learner. Learning never has to stop after you finish school. Anyone can continue to grow through a daily habit of reading. Subjects or specific areas of interest may change; we are all gifted in different areas, so as you go through the different seasons of life you will be attracted to different subjects.

This book of the law shall not depart out of your mouth; you shall meditate on it day and night, so that you may be careful to act in accordance with all that is written in it. For then you shall make your way prosperous, and then you shall be successful.

—JOSHUA 1:8 (NRSVCE)

Ask, and it will be given you; search, and you will find; knock, and the door will be opened for you. For everyone who asks receives, and everyone who searches finds, and for everyone who knocks, the door will be opened. Is there anyone among you who, if your child asks for bread, will give a stone? Or if the child asks for a fish, will give a snake? If you then, who are evil, know how to give good gifts to your children, how much more will your Father in heaven give good things to those who ask him!

In everything do to others as you would have them do to you; for this is the law and the prophets.

—MATTHEW 7:7-12 (NRSVCE)

A good alternative is to listen to audiobooks or watch videos about areas of interest. These aren't quite the same as reading a book, which is more tangible. You may have watched a movie that was based on a book. Most books use more detail and require more time and investment when reading, but this isn't always true. When watching videos or listening to audiobooks or podcasts, you can easily become distracted and miss a key message or main point. More senses—such as physical touch, sight, comprehension—are awakened when you hold a book in your hands and read it aloud or in your head. It certainly becomes more concrete.

CHAPTER 7

Connecting with Others and Building Relationships Through One Body

To connect with others and build relationships, focus on the other person more than on yourself. Good listening skills are key to building a connection. Mirroring a person's posture and using emotions that fit the topic are good ways to show a person that you are listening. Commenting on a few key phrases the person says lets them know you are truly present in conversation.

Limiting distraction is vital to connecting. Even if something happens outside your control, let the other person know that what they are saying is important. Explain that you have to complete your current task or take a small break and get back to the task. Afterward, be sure to reconnect to the topic where you left off, or ask the other person for a gentle reminder. Jotting a quick note can help you remember what was said, or add an item on your calendar if you make a commitment. You can also set notifications or send yourself reminders so you don't miss an event. Keeping track of important dates such as anniversaries, birthdays, holidays, or any other milestones of loved ones is also vital to building healthy and strong relationships.

Today we have many tools and resources to connect with others more personally. We have email, text messages, and social media at our fingertips. But the opportunity to connect in person, when possible, is always best, so that the other person not only can hear and see you, but can also bond through being physically present.

> Do nothing from selfish ambition or conceit, but in humility regard others as better than yourselves.
>
> —PHILIPPIANS 2:3 (NRSVCE)

Connecting with your children is essential for physical and mental growth, for both you and your child. Ways include active listening, staying present by limiting distractions, summarizing what was said, listening without interruptions, and most importantly avoiding judgment about what was said. Use physical touch, ask questions about their day while they were apart from you, and be certain to use eye contact, as it builds your interconnection. Show your kids how to connect and build relationships with others through communion with your spouse, local church, your child's school, sports, and hobbies. Above all, show them how to spend time with God, perhaps through Eucharistic Adoration.

> No one has ever seen God; if we love one another, God lives in us, and his love is perfected in us.
>
> —1 JOHN 4:12 (NRSVCE)

Recognizing and knowing your spouse and children's temperaments can help with positive interaction—and can also grow any other relationships. As God's children, we must strive to become more Christlike. When we work to grow and mature each day, our attitudes reflect strengths in our personalities. These allow us to let go of the weaknesses that affect our temper. Our personalities are who God intended us to be. Through the Sacrament of Reconciliation and frequent examination of conscience, reflecting prayerfully on our daily actions, feelings, and words, we invite the Holy Spirit into our lives.

Four Temperaments

Throughout the ages, scholars have identified four temperaments of human beings: choleric, melancholic, sanguine, and phlegmatic. We are not one-size-fits-all. It is good to meet people in their current state and approach each situation as needed. Most people have a predominant temperament that often complements a secondary one. You might even find yourself having elements of all four. In an article posted at the Good Catholic website (goodcatholic.com), Genevieve Netherton explained how knowing the four temperaments can help Catholics.

According to which temperament we have, there are certain sins we will tend to commit, and certain given virtues that will give us strength in seeking God.

The Choleric

- **Sins**—May struggle with anger, pride, and impatience. So he will need God's grace to cultivate gentleness, humility, and patience.
- **Virtues**—Usually has a strong will, great constancy, and energy for carrying out his tasks.

The Melancholic

- **Sins**—May struggle with being critical, moody, and despondent. He will need God's grace to cultivate joyful acceptance, selflessness, and hope.

- **Virtues**—Usually is compassionate, long-suffering, pious, and contemplative.

The Sanguine

- **Sins**—May struggle with superficiality, lust, and lack of perseverance. He will need God's grace to cultivate purity, interior depth and strength, and perseverance.
- **Virtues**—Usually is cheerful, generous, sincere, and sensitive to the suffering of others.

The Phlegmatic

- **Sins**—May struggle with laziness, the inability to confront or take initiative, and doing the wrong thing in order to please others. He will need God's grace to cultivate fortitude, holy ambition, and strength of will.
- **Virtues**—Usually is tranquil, full of common sense, assiduous, and almost immune to anger.

—Slightly adapted from Genevieve Netherton's "A Catholic Guide to the 4 Temperaments: Which One Are You?," Good Catholic, updated August 8, 2023, https://www.goodcatholic.com/a-catholic-guide-to-the-four-temperaments/

Stay in Good Air and Go the Distance

CHAPTER 8

Setting Realistic Goals Under the SMART Method

Creating goals can help you connect to your surroundings and building relationships.

Consider the SMART goal-setting system, which was articulated by George T. Doran in 1981.* SMART stands for *specific, measurable, attainable, relevant,* and *timely.*

For example, here were my SMART goals for writing this book:

- **Specific**—I will start prewriting this book in October 2023 and draft it by February 2024, After I send it out for revising, I will turn it in by March 2024 to the editor for publishing.

- **Measurable**—I will start my daily habit by investing a minimum of one hour each day, build a network through media tools, and obtain an editor for my book to be self-published.

---

* George T. Doran, "There's a S.M. A. R. T. Way to Write Management Goals and Objectives," *AMA Forum,* November 1981, accessed at https://community.mis.temple.edu/mis0855002fall2015/files /2015/10/S.M.A.R.T-Way-Management-Review.pdf.

- **Achievable**—I can achieve this goal by cutting back time on devices, stepping back from other commitments that don't serve my current focus toward writing my book, and asking close relationships for help with the mundane obstacles that fight for my attention.

- **Relevant**—I want to write my book to motivate other individuals to follow their calling through the marriage vocation of the Catholic Church.

- **Timely**—I will start prewriting in October after my wedding anniversary and then draft the manuscript by mid-February around my husband's birthday. Next I will send it for proofreading to my father, who agreed to get it done within a week, and send to my editor at FastEditing LLC. I will sign a contract by mid-March to self-publish the book through IngramSpark so it can be used to evangelize people and share the Good News of the Gospel.

Then the Lord answered me and said:
Write the vision;
    make it plain on tablets,
    so that a runner may read it.
For there is still a vision for the
      appointed time;
    it speaks of the end, and does not lie.

> If it seems to tarry, wait for it;
>   it will surely come, it will not delay.
>
> —HABAKKUK 2:2-3 (NRSVCE)

When setting goals, it is important to do something that is realistic and attainable. A good rule is to set goals that you can track daily, weekly, monthly, and yearly. Every bit of work adds up over a year of time. If you aren't tracking your goals, you won't be able to measure your strengths versus weaknesses.

Sometimes it can take a full year before you see improvement. But when you wait, great things come about. Patience is one of the fruits of the Holy Spirit. What matters most is not so much the size of a person's house or their number of children, but rather the attitude and heart of the person! We won't carry earthly things with us to the heavenly realms. Rather these relics, objects from an earlier time, are tools to help us in this life, and items we can share with others in need.

CHAPTER 9

Accomplishing More Than Ever

How does one stay self-disciplined in a world of busy distractions? One way to accomplish more than ever is to plan or review your calendar every evening ahead of the next day. This helps you keep focused on your task. Be sure to review your SMART goals to stay on target.

Take action today. Get moving, and stop overthinking. Ask yourself what you can do now or today to stay present with your focus. Even if you do something small, by doing small things you will get that momentum toward that dream. The future isn't guaranteed to anyone. All we have is the present moment, so make it count!

> Yet you do not even know what tomorrow
> will bring. What is your life? For you are
> a mist that appears for a little while and
> then vanishes.
>
> —JAMES 4:14 (NRSVCE)

> Prepare your work outside,
>   get everything ready for you in the field;
>   and after that build your house.
>
> —PROVERBS 24:27 (NRSVCE)

Be more like St. Therese the Little Flower, whose teaching portrayed how to trust more in God, even when we don't know where or how he is guiding us. She responded wholeheartedly with a desire to do good. Taking little actions toward others with great love, as she advocated, can transform one person's life—and gradually, perhaps, lead others to do the same across the globe. When you do small acts of kindness each day, your love can spread to others and become contagious.

Another way to accomplish more than ever is to create a daily routine or pattern involving the top things you want to change in your life. A good rule is to start small, picking no more than five things that you can realistically work toward daily. Whatever area you want to work on—for example, finances, marriage, relationships, health, interest in arts, science, or any other interest—decide what you wish to study. You might start small on your calendar by blocking off windows of time for tasks that you can realistically accomplish. You could start with 15 to 20 minutes every day to work toward your achievements. You could commit to reading a book on the area challenging you for 20 minutes each day, or maybe spend quality time with mentors who have accomplished similar goals. Whether you seek to increase your prayer life and meditation, practice gratitude, exercise daily, shift to healthier eating and meal portions, settle into a morning routine, or increase your sleep—whatever it might be, the hope is to build on the habit every day over time. When you plant the seeds, your garden will germinate. Be sure to reward yourself as you meet achievements through your daily wins.

Remember that doing new things can be a challenge. It isn't comforting to change. Fear can certainly prevent you from moving forward and taking action. Discipline is important to help you overcome any refusal to act and thereby avoid pain and suffering. Moving forward helps you take action and avoid being led astray by distraction, forgetfulness, or procrastination.

CHAPTER 10

Turning Goals into Reality Through Your Vocation in the Sacraments of the Church

Creating daily habits is essential for goal attainment. You might do something at the same time each day, do it first thing in the morning, or do it before you go to bed. A tracking device can help you ensure you're doing the new habit daily. Keep notes that you can look back on, whether on your phone or on good old-fashioned paper.

Finding a spiritual leader with success related to the goals you wish to strengthen is another good way to grow and hold yourself accountable. You can identify leads through networking and developing relationships. Now more than ever, you can connect with people across the globe through social media platforms, especially LinkedIn, where you can build a professional profile. On social media, it's valuable to connect with others on a personal level versus just responding to posts that others may see. Pick up the phone, meet in person when time allows, or continue the conversation in private messaging. You can have a lot of success in connecting with others in your area if you narrow your searches, saving time and travel expenses. When you find an advisor, be open to constructive criticism. Ask them about the best way to stay connected or good times to connect.

> Whatever you ask for in prayer with faith, you will receive.
>
> —MATTHEW 21:22 (NRSVCE)

We are living in a time when people have forgotten how to connect through in-person discussions. Today we use connection methods that give an instant response but fail to connect us through our senses. We use social media through digital devices, email, and text messaging. We have forgotten how to connect through personal contact.

Touch plays a vital role in communicating emotions to others. Studies have found that touch stimulates the body's production of oxytocin, which leads to bonding with others; the birthing process is known to elevate oxytocin levels, which promotes connection between mother and baby.

Whatever positive thoughts you're thinking in your head, be sure to act on them. Don't fall for the misconception that the other person knows what you're thinking. Reach out personally rather than just making assumptions. Picking up the phone and talking allows your tone of voice to be heard to avoid any confusion.

When in your community, connect with your surroundings. Talk to that person next to you at the store. Compliment them on a style of shirt you like or a helpful mannerism you see. This outreach helps build faith and brings us into wholeness.

These phrases might help you get started:

- "I like your outfit. It goes really well with your hair color." (Only say this if you truly believe it. The person will pick up if it's not genuine.)

- "That was really nice that you had your child step to the side so I could walk by."

- "I appreciate how you waited and let me go first."

- "Thank you for serving me today." (Even if they had to do it for work, a word of thanks helps them feel appreciated.)

- "How nice of you to bring your kids with you and teach them social interaction that shows what way they should go."

- "It was thoughtful of you to let that person go in front who only had a few items."

- "Thanks for helping the older person with something they needed. I'm sure they really appreciated that."

"Not everyone who says to me, 'Lord, Lord,' will enter the kingdom of heaven, but only the one who does the will of my Father in heaven. . . . Everyone then who hears these words of mine and acts on them will be like a wise man who built his house on rock. The rain fell, the floods came, and the winds blew and beat on that house, but it did not fall, because it had been founded on rock. And everyone who hears these words of mine and does not act on them will be like a foolish man who built his house on sand. The rain fell, and the floods came, and the winds blew and beat against that house, and it fell—and great was its fall!" Now when Jesus had finished saying these things, the crowds were astounded at his teaching, for he taught them as one having authority, and not as their scribes.

—MATTHEW 7:21, 24-29 (NRSVCE)

When you truly follow the teachings of the Church, God will sweep you off your feet. He gives himself to us in the form of a small host that looks like—but isn't just—a piece of bread. What seems to be just a piece of bread is his very Body! He wants you to unify with his divine nature through the Holy Spirit. This is why Eucharistic Adoration and daily Mass are so incredibly extraordinary, in addition to contemplative prayer, in helping you draw close to Jesus.

We are all growing at different rates and facing different storms. Our journey here is to help one another reach the other side. It is extremely important to be connected with your surroundings and to shine your light. You never know who you might help out of a place of darkness. We don't know what goes on in the mind of somebody else. Sometimes on the outside, any one of us can seem like we have it all put together—but that appearance doesn't mean that we aren't in a storm hoping for the sun to shine and a rainbow to appear!

The seven sacraments of the Church—Baptism, Confirmation, Eucharist, Reconciliation, Anointing of the Sick, Holy Orders, and Matrimony—were passed on by Jesus to the Apostles. They are channeled to us in the present day through the Holy Spirit to bring grace upon us and allow us to grow in joy.

Beloved, let us love one another, because love is from God; everyone who loves is born of God and knows God. Whoever does not love does not know God, for God is love. God's love was revealed among us in this way: God sent his only Son into the world so that we might live through him. In this is love, not that we loved God but that he loved us and sent his Son to be the atoning sacrifice for our sins. Beloved, since God loved us so much, we also ought to love one another. No one has ever seen God; if we love one another, God lives in us, and his love is perfected in us.

—1 JOHN 4:7-12 (NRSVCE)

Blessing to all those living

the marriage sacrament!

Prayers for Marriage and
the Honor of Parenting

Lord, I pray for our marriage to always be protected and hand it over to you in wherever you lead us. I trust in what you have in store. Let your will be done so we can model to others what unification looks like in our vocation. Through our oath to you in the marriage sacrament of sickness and health until death do us part. Welcome us to heaven upon our departures from this life.

Lord, I pray that our child/children call on you as their savior. Fill them with your truths and protect them all the days of their life. Let them come to forgiveness of past wrongs and be healed through your gift of grace. Welcome them into heaven after this life. Let your will be done!

Above all build your faith through daily contemplative prayer in addition to formal prayers. This can be done by setting our hearts and minds through a calm, quiet, motionless state of stillness by resting in God's presence.

For Further Reading

Focus on the Family: https://www.focusonthefamily .com/pro-life/is-abortion-a-sin

For Your Marriage: https://www.foryourmarriage.org

Heartbeat International: https://www.heartbeat international.org/

Marriage Enrichment: https://www.usccb.org/ topics/marriage-and-family-life-ministries/ marriage-enrichment

National Right to Life: https://nrlc.org/

Parents and Parenting: https://www.usccb.org /topics/marriage-and-family-life-ministries /parents-and-parenting

Right to Life of Michigan: https://rtl.org/find -help/post-abortion/

Strong Catholic Family Faith: https://www. catholicfamilyfaith.org/

About the Author

Heidi resides in a township of fewer than 6,000 people in the heart of Michigan near Lake Huron with her beloved husband, Paul; children Devy, Kinley, and Liam; and a guardian angel daughter, Annabelle, who watches from above. She holds an MS degree in human services. Heidi absolutely cherishes the outdoors and being in the presence of her loved ones near and far. All of you know who you are, even if we haven't connected in years! She loves conquering new challenges. Some of her passionate practices include worshiping our Lord; praying forgiveness for the past, present, and future generations; spending quality time with family; reading books; dancing and moving; being on and near the water; exploring new areas; listening to the sounds of nature; surrounding herself with others; helping where she can; and of course writing!

To connect with Heidi, send any inquiries to heidiarnone@gmail.com.

Visit the book website to learn more: https://heidiarnone.wixsite.com/dklforever.

Or connect with Heidi and follow her on LinkedIn: https://www.linkedin.com/in /heidi-arnone-291971233

NOTES

NOTES

NOTES

ENDORSEMENTS FOR HEIDI ARNONE

"Heidi is a passionate and purposeful leader . . . Her intentionality is incredible! I rarely see a leader who combines a focus to get things done with high impact relational skills—Heidi is one of those elite people!"

—LYLE WELLS, PRESIDENT AT INTEGRUS
LEADERSHIP, SENIOR PASTOR AT FIRST
FRANKLIN IN FRANKLIN, TEXAS, AND
AUTHOR AND KEYNOTE SPEAKER

"After seeing Heidi work hard to start, build, and scale her own business, here's what I learned about her . . . Heidi is tenacious in her pursuit of personal, professional, and leadership development but it's her heart to help people that I find to be one of her best attributes. She has a passion to see marriages and families thrive and she's willing to do everything in her power to help people."

—ANDREW TIDWELL, TIDWELL &
COMPANY, LLC, BUSINESS COACH